SITA'S SISTERS

SITA'S SISTERS

Sanjukta Dasgupta

HAWAKAL

HAWAKAL

Published by Hawakal Publishers
185 Kali Temple Road, Nimta, Kolkata 700049
India

Email info@hawakal.com
Website www.hawakal.com

First edition November, 2019

Copyright © Sanjukta Dasgupta 2019

Cover art: shutterstock
Cover design: Bitan Chakraborty

All rights reserved. No part of this publication may be reproduced or transmitted (other than for purposes of review/critique) in any form or by any means, electronic or mechanical, including photocopy, recording, or any information storage and retrieval system without prior permission in writing from the publisher or the copyright holder where applicable. The author asserts her moral right to be identified as the author of her work.

ISBN: 978-93-87883-89-5

Price: INR 300 | USD 11.99

DEDICATION

This book is for all my young poet friends, students and scholars who have instilled in me the courage and confidence to express my stress and distress, my hopes and dreams, my trials and triumphs.

Sanjukta Dasgupta
September 28, 2019

ACKNOWLEDGEMENT

I wish to record my unbounded gratitude to my gracious publisher and young poet friend Dr. Kiriti Sengupta for his kind support, expertise and care in publishing this book.

In 2017, he had published my fifth book of poems *Lakshmi Unbound.*

CONTENTS

Sita's Sisters	13
Sita's Lament	15
Sita and the Golden Deer	17
Sita meets Lakshmi	19
Kind Karuna	20
Binary	21
The Pillion Rider	23
Kali	25
Why I am a Feminist	27
Emptiness	30
Heaven on Earth	32
Valley of Fear	34
O My God	35
My Mother's Harmonium	36
Though	39
Easter in Krakow	40
Park Street	42
Hunger	43
Have Oil expect Turmoil	45
A Failed Dream	47
Auschwitz: Hell on Earth	48
DumDum	50

Texting vs Meeting	51
What's Poetry	53
Moon and I	54
That night	55
Autumn	57
Topic of Cancer	58
Calcutta/Kolkata	60
Two in one Calcutta	61
Cows Blazing	62
Balloon	64
The Dumb Cow	66
The Hunted	68
Why I am not a Humanist	70
Who Killed the little tribal girl?	72
One Hundred and Fifty Years Young	74
Protest	76
Dress and Address	77
Dhoti Dance	78

A Preamble...

Though it's customary to regard any creative piece, primarily poetry as a spontaneous overflow of powerful feelings, those who write poems also know about an indomitable compulsion that forces the poet to translate her thoughts and feelings into the words we use for human communication and sharing of cognitive processes.

In selecting *Sita's Sisters* as the title poem of my sixth volume of poetry, I feel the battle for gender equality and gender justice will have to go on, in a resolute and concerted manner, till the battle is won, no matter how long it may take. After all, not unlike a man, a woman can be destroyed but not defeated.

Unfortunately, the more technologically advanced we are becoming, a reverse and regressive mode of barbarism, violence, hatred, intolerance, deception, greed for power and profit seem to have vitiated the entire world, both physical and virtual. The era of globalization has generated unprecedented egocentricity, unethical practices, human trafficking, threats of nuclear war, organized and often state-sponsored terrorism, mass exodus of refugees and asylum seekers, fake news and unscrupulousness in using divinity and organized religion as tools of exploitation and elimination of targeted individuals, groups and communities.

In my fifth book of poems *Lakshmi Unbound*, published in 2017, I had humbly ventured to state that my poems can be read as poems of resistance, but I would like to revise that statement in my sixth book *Sita's Sisters* and urge my readers to read these poems as texts of resistance and resilience, confidently gesturing towards inevitable social change.

The representations of Sita in Hindu religious texts often depict her as the avatar or incarnation of the Goddess Lakshmi, the consort of Lord Vishnu. Therefore, perhaps it is in the fitness of textual juxtaposition that *Lakshmi Unbound* as a poetic text will be followed by the evolutionary exploration of Sita and her innumerable sisters, who still suffer in silence but yet surprisingly use silence as an effective tool of resistance and resilience. I strongly believe that through strategies of peaceful resistance the Sitas of the world shall overcome their humiliation someday. Hopefully in the near future!

Sita's Sisters

Sita's sister was a good woman
She belonged to just one man
Marriage, vermilion powder, bangles
Dangled from her slender arms
Her husband was her God,
Her Lord and Master
Her stifled breath, her sealed lips
He was the fierce tiger she the gentle lamb
Eye contact was a total taboo
"How dare you stare at me " he roared
"I'll scoop out your eyes you brazen wife"

Sita's countless sisters- what were their names?
Rita, Mita, Arpita, Sumita, Rinita
Lolita, Bonita, Anita, Sunita, Sucheta...

Thousands and thousands of Sita's sisters
Programmed parrots
Pathetic puppets
Remote controlled robots

Sita's sisters watched in silence
Sita's sisters were deaf and dumb

Sita's Sisters

Sita's sisters shut their eyes
Sita's sisters had eyeless holes
Sita's sisters cried out to their Mother Earth
"Remember our sister Sita's suicide,
 Innocent Sita's traumatic trials
O mother rescue us as you rescued Sita"

But alas the earth did not split open for Sita's sisters
The incessant unbearable cries of Sita's sad sisters
Had turned their Mother Earth to senseless stone!

Sita's Lament

I wish I was a girl again
Playing in my mother's garden
I wish I could climb trees
I wish I could pluck hanging fruits
I wish I did not have to stoop
To pick fruits lying under trees
Fallen flowers, roots and shoots

I wish I was free to run off with the golden deer
I wish I could spread my arms like a bird and fly away
I wish I could run through acres of green fields
I wish I could plunge into the flowing river
And swim alongside a sailing boat
I wish I could disobey and stray far away

I wish my two boys could love me
As they love their father
About whom they have only heard
But have not seen from the day
They arrived on this good earth
But Luva and Kusha long for their father
Ram is their hero, their role model

Me, Sita, their devoted mother
I could never be their role model

I could never inspire them
They found nothing motivational
They found nothing inspirational
They found nothing aspirational
About me, their devoted, abandoned, exiled mother Sita

Shunning further exhibitions of pristine, pious purity
I have now entered my mother's healing bosom
To be a queen had been traumatic and beyond all reason!

Sita and the Golden Deer

The forest was green
The sky was blue
Sita rambled through the brambles
Sita stumbled on a golden deer
It ran off trembling with fear
Sita cried out, "nothing to fear, dear little deer"
But the golden deer raced like an arrow out of fear
The golden deer was terrified by Sita's greedy cheer

Being a good wife Sita asked Ram,
The exiled king of Kosala
'Bring me the golden deer
That has run off trembling with fear'
Obediently Ram ran after the deer
He had nothing to fear
From a sweet golden deer
Which from a distance
Seemed so cherubic and dear

But as Ram was late
Sita stood at the gate
She asked Lakshman to find out
As Ram didn't respond to their shouts

Lakshman went in search of Ram, his brother
He drew a charmed circle around Sita like a mother
But it was an unlucky day for everyone
Except scheming Ravana who tricked and took Sita hostage
Took Sita to Lanka and held her in bondage
Tearful, fearful, her plight worse than the golden deer
Sita wept in misery, Sita wept in fear

After all, Sita like everywoman was the root of all evil
Whether it was Helen of Troy, Draupadi or Eve
That men can be evil, no one would ever believe

Male authors of the world's patriarchal epics blame
The bewitching femme fatales who seem bereft of shame
But the heroes insist they need such beauties as their brides
In the killing fields and theatres of war, like trophies
                                        by their sides.

Sita Meets Lakshmi

"Are you Lakshmi"
Asked Sita as the dazzling goddess
Ran like the golden deer
But stopped at once as Sita called.

"O dear Goddess Lakshmi
How did you dare step out of doors
Are you not the one
Who is eternally bound to hearth and home?"

Lakshmi smiled
A mischievous twinkle lit her eyes
"I am not Lakshmi Bound
I am Lakshmi Unbound
Come Sita, join me if you can
Of course you can, some say you are me!"

A storm rose all around
A storm rose in Sita's heart
Sita stepped out
To step into her own being
Sita felt Lakshmi's firm clasp
As her chains clattered to the ground!

Note: It is widely believed that Sita is the avatar, incarnation or manifestation of the Goddess Lakshmi.

Kind Karuna

Kind and gentle Karuna was Sita's sister
For long she was nursing a puffy blister
As it was on her ankle the blister like a bubble
Caused Karuna no trouble
No one knew Karuna had cancer
No one asked, so Karuna never answered

Till one day silently the bubble burst
As she cried in pain their words were like knife thrusts
'No doctor for you wicked woman with a womb full of girl seeds
Just bear the pain or die for your evil misdeeds'
The three daughters of Karuna clung to their mother
Pouring kerosene on them said their father,
"You must go, all of you, so that we can live
We have no need for a girl producing womb
We need sons, not daughters like poison bombs"

Late that night a furious gust of wind
Raised the ashes from their charred bodies skywards
Perhaps towards peace and home!

Binary

After the departure
Of the ten-armed Goddess of deliverance
Arrives the soft, submissive angel in the house
The alluring Lakshmi the goddess of home and hearth
Peace, prosperity, piousness
Radiates as Lakshmi reposes on a blossoming lotus

But the decks have to be cleared
For the grand arrival of Goddess Lakshmi
An effigy of an ugly rag doll named Alakshmi
Is thrashed with sadistic ecstasy
Its severed head, arms and legs
Brutally swept out of the premises
By broom brandishing virile home guards
"Get out Alakshmi
Let not your evil shadow pollute
Our home. Get out of our sight you
Self-willed, impudent, defiant
Inauspicious, argumentative witch!"

On the full-moon night
The earth was dripping in glowing golden light

At midnight Lakshmi entered the waiting homes
The priest trembled. He thought he heard Lakshmi say,
"Alakshmi and Lakshmi are immortal
Siamese twins my mortal kin"

Note: Alakshmi may be regarded as the antonym of the domestic goddess Lakshmi. Lakshmi is worshipped as a domestic Goddess of family harmony, prosperity and peace and is regarded as a role model for all good and dutiful Hindu women.

Alakshmi is a deconstructive symbol of all that is considered to be essential attributes of good and dutiful women. Alakshmi therefore can be interpreted as a home-breaker, a destructive evil force that rocks the foundations of traditional practices. Alakshmi claims identity, independence and respectful recognition. Alakshmi as symbol and metaphor is therefore considered to be a threat to the patriarchal establishment.

The Pillion Rider

No one taught me driving
No one gave me a bike
They said, "he has a bike
So what's your problem you silly wife?"

So lifelong I am a pillion rider
No one asked me
Do you like to sit behind him
Are you scared, are you terrified
Do you want a helmet too
But a helmet for me he just won't buy.

Though I am the driver in his kitchen
They call me a cook
Is that a common noun or a command
Cook Cook Cook
Endlessly chopping, churning, cooking
I know the kitchen is his,
The chopping knife is his
Everything belongs to him
Every plate, every spoon, every bin
As my body too belongs to him

Why am I so poor dear Goddess Lakshmi
I tried to follow all your rules
Fasted steadfastly for the moon to rise
Though I can't stand pangs of hunger and thirst
Lakshmi Devi in you in trust
My silks and jewellery are not mine
Nothing is mine not even me.
My body is used by him
My body is abused by him
I have no desire, no will, no wish
I am just a poor pillion Rider

I am just a pillion rider
I am just a pillion rider
I can only be directed and driven
I can't be trusted to direct and drive
I can only drive myself crazy
Riding on this dreadful pillion seat
Holding or not holding the callous shoulders
Ahead of me
Not knowing anymore
Whether I am at all able
Or permanently disabled-
A pillion rider on a lifelong traumatic ride

Kali

Her jet black flying tresses
Like dark monsoon clouds
A bright black halo lit up her dusky face
Her dark eyes were blood shot with angst and grief
Her lolling tongue perhaps a thrust of self-control

Like a timeless ebony sculpture
Her dazzling stark dark silken form
Stood statuesque
On her supine intimate partner

She was a furious doer
She was a restless dreamer
She was a tempest, a tornado
She was the ruthless Redeemer
She was not Bhadrakali
She was Chamunda Kali the relentless slayer
She was Kali who haunted the burning ghats
Shamshan Kali, the ultimate liberator

A garland of skulls around her neck
Gruesome, grotesque and gorgeous
A scintillating scimitar in one raised hand

The other left arm gripping the hair of a severed head
Her two right arms aloft in a gesture of assurance
Four-armed Kali the Mother of all Avengers
Stood tall and stark and very dark
An invincible symbol of power and trust

A towering terrifying terminator
Raging like a mother of all tsunamis
Goddess Kali restlessly rushes on
In pursuit of the demons of deceit and lust
The world feels secure as caregiver Kali
Paces the earth like a prowling panther
Tireless vigilante!

Why I am a Feminist

Feminism is hated because women are hated. Anti-feminism is a direct expression of misogyny; it is the political defense of women hating.

While gossip among women is universally ridiculed as low and trivial, gossip among men, especially if it is about women, is called theory, or idea, or fact.

Seduction is often difficult to distinguish from rape. In seduction, the rapist often bothers to buy a bottle of wine.

Andrea Dworkin from Woman Hating

In my father's home
My mother and I
Lived and loved
We sang, read books
Danced in the living room
My father, my mother's husband
Was a friend in need for both of us

A brilliant mentor, a candid counsellor
Though he had been a freedom fighter
Male braggadocio was not his style

Gender fluidity made us hold our heads high
Our minds were without fear within the home

The world was a different eyeball game
As I grew up, stares, winks, slurping noises
Made me walk faster to reach home
Guys would brush past in their bikes
Guys would push if not pull at will
Guys would press against me in a bus
Guys would use language that I hadn't heard before

The boyfriends swung between lust and love
Commitment phobic straight guys
Totally confused alternatives
Youth was a time of great expectations
Youth was a time of great disillusionments
Youth was a time of trust deficit
Youth was a time of emotional bankruptcy
Youth was the time of trauma and hypocrisy
Youth was when patriarchy threw of its mask and cloak

The male-stream dominated the mainstream
Though half the human race was female alas!
Female-stream was about shock, sadness, fears and tears
She became an uncared for caregiver
Serving a life term in the prison cell
Rigorous imprisonment 24x7
In the deadlock of wedlock

The gates of patriarchy flung open
The gates of patriarchy devoured desire
The gates of patriarchy

Snuffed out all dreams and targets
Patriarchy encouraged misogynists
Remember Sita, Draupadi,
Hirimba and Sakuntala at home
Remember Penelope, Desdemona,
Ophelia and Hermoine in the world

Discriminated, assaulted, insulted, humiliated
Raped everywhere, even within marriage
Slaving in the kitchen, slaving in bed
Slaving to be a good woman
Slaving to make a happy family
Slaving to seem self-sacrificing
Slaving to be crowned Angel in the House
Slaving to be praised as Lakshmi
A nerveless Nora, an anorexic Barbie doll
In the home of pusillanimous prigs

If only I had eyes which could not see
If only I had ears that could not hear
If only I had a mind that couldn't think
If only I had a heart that couldn't feel
If only I had been a puppet on a string
A robot, an Alexa, a programmed AI performer
Definitely then I would not have been a feminist!

Emptiness

Emptiness
Envelopes and engulfs
Loneliness
Tortures and torments
Silence
Howls voicelessly
Hyenas
Stare snarl snigger
Insane
Leopards leap and cavort
In the mind's circus

From being
To not-being
From life
To lifelessness
A dark shadow
Like a mesh of
Dark clouds
Shuts out all light
Emptiness
Roars like a monarch

In an empty palace
A palace of illusions
With ten thousand empty rooms

The blind king in his palace
Of ten thousand rooms
Walks, runs, strolls,
Limps through spaces
Spaces without names
Spaces without identity
Like a vapid void
Of no consequence
Emptiness is a torture chamber

Yet and yet, a persistent flower
Spreads its fragile petals
Through the thin crack in the wall...

Heaven on Earth

That was the mistake
A divine mistake
Made by the infallible creator
Instead of a heaven out of reach
Here was heaven within reach
A Heaven on earth!

Such easy access
Made the salivating hell hounds
Tear hungrily through the luscious green
The sparkling, dancing mountain rivers
Became rivers of blood
The valley became a vale of tears

Severed limbs bounced up
In the swift streaming currents
A final farewell gesture
Here fair was foul
Here foul was fair
Here the pristine snow
Turned black and blue
Like whiplash stripes

Heaven wept
As its twin on earth
So close to the heavens
So close to the home
Of the divine dignitaries
Helplessly battled
Multiple organ failure
Incessant haemorrhage
Visible and invisible
Internal and external
Alas! our heaven on earth
Far worse than hell!

The Valley of Fear

Suddenly out of the blue
A metal mesh spread like a tent
Over everyone and everything
There were boots on every inch
Of the green and glorious valley

"Why, why , why"
They wailed and writhed
"let us be free, let us breathe
We are not criminals
We are citizens like all others"

The gods in the towers
The gods in the seats of power
Said, " Its for your own good
Just follow our will
And you will dazzle and shine
As we marry your girls
And buy your land"

The valley of fear
A valley of pyramids
A burial ground
With no mourners
A rocky wasteland
Of debris and bones!

O My God

Our Father where are you
Your kingdom is swamped with imposters
Thy will is not done on earth
The will of Satan rules heads and hearts
There is no one to give us our daily needs
The Seven Deadly Sins make us bleed
Forgive our vacillation, forgive our trepidation
Silence the trespassers, silence the oppressors
Silence the stranglers of freedom
Silence the devilish tempters
We have just one fervent prayer
Deliver us from these demons of evil!
For thine is the kingdom, power and glory
Don't forgive them for they are never sorry!

My Mother's Harmonium

In the corner of our busy corridor
The silent harmonium
Sat in a dark box
Like a boulder

"My five year old son loves harmoniums
He plays an imaginary harmonium
By tapping on the table
A hair comb as bellows"

We had forgotten
That my mother's harmonium
Sat in the corner of the corridor
Silent and still

We searched the attic
For my mother's harmonium
During periodic clearance drives
Did someone give it away

Or did it go away
In a junk sale-

A strange pain
Stabbed my mind

Then suddenly
Like a vision
The neglected boulder on the long corridor
Flashed on the mind-screen–
There indeed sat my mother's harmonium

Silent, smiling, as it was
Lifted out of the box after many years
The white reeds now chrome yellow
The dark auburn harmonium was
Released in the fresh air

Trapped in a dark wooden coffin for years
My mother's harmonium resurrected
Will begin a new journey tomorrow
As it reaches the five year old's home

Tonight on the old harmonium
I will let my fingers play the old tunes
That my mother and I used to sing together
The harmonium had once travelled
To many function halls

My mother was always more at ease
Singing while playing her own harmonium
Or accompanying me as I sang alone or with her
As we did the last time we were together
Before she had to go away forever

Tomorrow, my mother will guide
The tender fingers of the five year old
As he plays my mother's harmonium

As she had once guided the fingers
Of her own daughter when she was five

Tonight however
I'll play the farewell song
On my mother's harmonium

Though...

Though we slept in the same bed for years
You dreamt of hills, I dreamt of the seven seas
Though we woke up together in the soft morning light
You just wanted tea I wanted a new world
Though we took trams, trains and cars for work
Your cell phone was active yet mute,
Mine was about vibrating sound
Though we watched movies together
You liked the brain-brawn combo
I was hooked to love stories
Though we ate together every day at home
Or cafes or in restaurants
I mostly ate what you liked as I grew to like them too
Though we wore what we liked,
I knew what you liked you never did
Our incessant meetings at intersections
Laughed at our parallel routes
As we held hands and
Our entwined fingers spoke in silent dialogue.

Easter in Krakow

There's a church outside my window
The church bells toll through the days and nights
Calling, warning, reminding
As church goers flock up the steps
In rain, hail, snow, sunshine
The House of God beckons
As children, parents, grandparents
Youngsters and the very old
All walk to church

They flock to church with serious devotion
Leaves on Palm Sunday
Easter baskets On Easter Saturday
Blessed with sprinkles Of Holy Water
Easter Sunday seems radiant and rosy
As the church bells ring joyously
In the rain, on a cloudy Easter Sunday

What if it is raining
Easter with its promise of new life
The light rain like gentle holy water
Sprinkled from the vigilant Heaven
Where we must all return, Prince and Pauper,

Priests and Politicians
Kings and Beggars, Haves and Have-nots
Returning to the One who was killed
Only to be resurrected and restored
Like the temporary annihilation
Of Truth by Evil
Like the resurrection of Truth from the
Swirling sewerages of evil serpentine...

Park Street

"That school on Park Street is so beautiful"
The awestruck student told her teacher
The nun of her missionary school replied
"we are all missionaries
But their school is for the rich
Our school is for the poor"
The student rushed back to her parents
"Our school is for the poor, sister said
Who are the rich, what do they do
I know they read the same books
Do the same exams as we do
But they must be dressed in silks in summer
Eating biriyani all the time"

No buses plied on Park Street
No rickshaws, the chariots of fire
No bicycles, no hawkers
Bystanders and busy pedestrians
Lined the pavements stretched
In front of magic names and heavy doors
Guards guarded those doors that swung open
For the rich, slammed shut for the poor
No parking on Park Street for the poor
It was a seductive street that ravished the rich
And humiliated the poor!

Hunger

The Super 30s
Need sparkling water
To coax hunger for the next gourmet meal
The Loser 70s
Need just any water, from pond or tap
To comfort hunger pangs, their lifelong handicap!

The superstars shine and belch
The losers wince and quench
Their thirst, cupping water from roadside taps-
"Food, food, give us food, any food
We want to live, to live we must have food"

Suddenly last night
Someone waved a magic wand
The loser 70s found at dawn
Plates and plates of pasta and pizza
Mutton biriyani and paneer tikka
Fish and chips and chocolate truffle cakes
Fruit juices and creamy milk shakes.

The aromatic fragrance of food,
A rare double bonanza

The eager loser 70s reached for the plates
But their tongues rebelled, repelled by the tastes
Of the gourmet style Super30 delicacies
They threw up the cheesy pasta and pizza
Instead of the bizarre superfood of Paradise
They begged for a bowl of steaming rice
As they were truly hungry
And not bored to death about the same old food!

Have Oil, Expect Turmoil

The Oil Wells of the world sighed and wept
The wail of the wells startled the oil crooks
They were organized invisible miners
Scouring every corner of the good earth
For everybody's oil but their own
Creating killing fields along the ancient rivers
The Tigris, the Euphrates, the Nile
None were safe from such satanic greed

They were the insatiable oil sharks
The Godzillas of greed the sneering gargoyles
Who just never would leave the world in peace
All who did not submit were diabolic dictators
Iraq and Libya were pulverized
Chad, Somalia, Yemen, Iran
Afghanistan, North Korea and Syria
Could just catch their fragile breath
And no one can ever forget the not so oily Vietnam.

Then the sharks suddenly rushed South
Their nuclear jaws wide open, ready for the kill

But the poor, starving people
Of the southern hemisphere did not relent
The grinning green notes from the North
Lured and lurked and tempted every one

But their talisman was their path-finder
He lived in their hearts,
He lived in their minds
He lived in their dreams

They made paper planes out of the green power notes
Green notes were showered on their bodies
Power Notes slithered into their homes
Like green slimy snakes through the porous borders
The green notes looked jaundiced and pestilence-stricken
As the proud people erected
The invincible wall of resistance
Built with bricks of love and dedication
Built with strong steel shafts of courage and conviction

In death he lived on more and more
His was the brand name
Tattooed on every heart and mind
"we shall overcome" they thundered
Far, far away the ground shook
Under the feet of the depraved Satanic gang
Like bedevilled dominoes they slipped
Tumbled and fell again!

A Failed Dream
(With sincere apologies to Rabindranath Tagore)

Where the mind is full of fear and the head hangs down
Where Knowledge is controlled
Where the world is broken into tiny cruel fragments
By narrow domestic walls
Where words spill out from the dark depths of untruth
Where tireless endeavours strive towards diabolic oppression
Where the clear stream of reason is
Clogged with glutinous effluents
The dreary wasteland of dead habit is all around
Where the mind is trapped in serpentine gyres of malice
Hatching more and more Satanic thought and action
Into that Hell of horror, O Unfortunate citizens,
Let not my country dive!

Auschwitz:Hell on Earth

From Krakow to Auschwitz
A ride of 65 miles
Less than 2 hours away by bus
Yet Krakow to Auschwitz
Is a devastating journey
From serene Heaven
To the abysmal depths of Hell

From the humane to the bestial
From radiance of mercy
To the ruthlessness of planned murder
The Entry Gate to this man-made Hell
Declared in oracular promise "work sets you free"
The treachery of rhetoric!

It is not about Holocaust tourism
It is not a simulacra of horror spectacle
It is about the horrendous inhumanity
Of the relentless racist human race
A spectacle of cruelty
In every encased space
Shoes, clothes, boxes

Books, pages, personal cherished gifts
Toys, balls, dolls and infinite others
Till a pyramid of shoes shock and stun

Traumatized tourists troop out of Auschwitz
Pervaded by an indescribable horrific gloom
How human perversity for power and profit
Destroyed thousands and thousands and thousands
Of grandparents, parents, mothers, daughters
Girls, boys, brothers, fathers, husbands, fiancées
Endless processions of branded humans
Seduced, coerced or thrust
Into the ghastly gas chambers

Auschwitz warns every visitor from
All parts of the rainbow world
Never again, never again, never again
Commit the same mistake
In the Name of God!

DumDum

It is from where airplanes fly out
To desired distant destinations
It is where thousands deplane every day
To enter the city of Kolkata
Dumdum the gateway to Kolkata
Enfolds in its history
Robert Clive's abode
The Heritage Clive House
Now a heap of crumbling walls and pillars

Robert Clive, the first British military officer
Launched the East India Company by hook or crook
Siraj ud dullah the monarch
Succumbed sadly to his sly Anglo tricks
And Clive flew the Union Jack on Indian soil

The gun and shell factory, the armoury
The wide roads, the large mansions of Zamindars
The green trees, the green ponds, the canals
The military cantonment and the rising and landing
Of steel birds in rhythm with the high-flying kites
Circling the blue sky in the blazing sun
The shrill screech of kites unlike the drone of airplanes
A signpost of history, a landmark where the world
Meets and departs, politicians, profiteers and poets
All continue to set their foot on the soil of Dumdum!

Texting vs Meeting

Now more often texting
Seems so serene and secure
A small rectangle in the palm
Conveys hope, despair
Problems, trials , triumphs

Meeting face to face
Seems a cruel diversion
Like a panoptic x ray eye...
My eyes focus on the stubble on your chin
The tired eyes, the wrong shade of lipstick
The bad teeth as you smile
The cheap accessories that you wear
The retail shop clothes and shoes
That cover you but expose your class

The way you munch meat,
Sip your fresh lime soda
Cough, sneeze, forget the right word
And become bi-lingual
Your untrimmed nails, your dry skin
Cracks and fractures on both our faces
Facing each other

Texting sustains romance
Imagination is triggered
As the chosen words
Either facts or fake
Often in a mode of
Self-dramatization
A dialogic monologue
Reaching out
Reaching in

Texting is
Selective life
Restful, illusory
Meeting is unbearable
Jabs of cruel reality!
Hide, hide, hide
Hide and text
Maybe that's best!

Note: Texting essentially started in the 1920s when RCA Communications (known today as Verizon Wireless) in New York City first introduced the telex service. The first text messages were sent from New York to London via RCA's transatlantic circuits.

Today, text messaging is often used by mobile phone users as an alternate method of communicating when voice communication is difficult, inappropriate or undesirable. In other instances, sending a text message is less expensive. It's also less intrusive because the receiver can attend to the message at his or her leisure.

https://www.techopedia.com/definition/15108/texting

What's Poetry

Where's the poetry
Asked the young poet
It's so prosaic
No flights of fancy
No wingless doves
No leaping leopards
No Christ the Tiger
Just peacocks
Who no longer dance
Monsoon is just a trickle
Slimy water running
Into sewers of spite
Swirling like a whirlpool
Sucking poetry
Into its timeless tunnel
As the binaries embrace
And free verse is born!

Moon and I

In fact we are buddies
Moon and I
We share a close bond
Closer than a child to the mother
Closer than the leaves to flowers
Moon and I
Buddies forever
We light each other
With reflected light

Moon and I
Lonely in our dark orbits
Till he arrives in his chariot
His horses breathing heavily
He smiles at us
And we glimmer and glow
As we reflect his light

Moon and I
Buddies forever
In dense darkness
Or borrowed light
"Appalling" smirks Apollo
"What a sightless light"!

That Night

That night
That late night
Just a minute before midnight
The hair on my skull
Raised itself like a wig
It floated in mid-air
Like a grisly flying saucer

That night
That late night
Just a minute before midnight
My skull split open
Like a knifed watermelon
A strange labour surge
Cracked open my bald pate

That night
That late night
Just a minute before midnight
Strange unhinging and heaving within
My skull cracked open
Among the coils and cells inside

There was a cheeky grey cell
That revolved like a trained ballerina

Someone whispered
It's a cerebral stroke
Just before the stroke of midnight
Not a cracked skull
That had split wide open
Stealthily someone stroked the
Crunchy, juicy, red innards
So like a split watermelon
 I sank and sank and sank
And then zoomed out of sight
As the world spun around
In a furious tandava
That startled Lord Shiva
As he eyed his dizzily spinning
Cosmic competitor!

Autumn

I have now left Spring far behind
Autumn now holds my veined hands
In a tender grip
As I snuggle in an autumnal embrace
I now know
If Autumn comes
Winter can't be far behind.

Spring sprang surprises and shocks
The magical monsoon healed and mellowed
Strands of silver brightened my hair
With unwelcome persistent care
Autumn now is in my eyes
Cataracts and dripping tears
Well up and stream,
Though I no longer cry

Spring now seems to have been
Bubbling with mirth and lies
Autumn prepares me with compassion
For the everlasting hibernation
For Winter now tip toes close behind.

Topic of Cancer

The Monarch of malignancy
Reigns in every nook and cranny
Of the accursed pitiful nation
The Emperor of all Maladies marches
Masculine, regal, megalomaniac
Power lies in the embrace of authority
Poisonous power that implodes silently
Melanoma, leukemia, lymphoma
Endless fearsome names
Cheered by the monomaniac

This emperor enters in silence
Casts the carcinogenic seeds within
The unsuspecting, defenceless rag and bone house
The emperor waits with patience and glee
As the seeds sprout, the saplings wave slimy tentacles
The white cells breed like maggots
A white Lycra bodysuit
Stretching over a skeletal frame

The carcinogenic creepers climb up the throat
Enter wherever it can wriggle through

Into the uterus, into the bones
Wrapping the lungs and pancreas
The mammary glands and all red cells
Seals the lips, seals the eyes, seals the ears
With teeming tumours, dripping and sore
The evil emperor reigns over all
In cruel and cold indifference
As is the wont of all kings of course!

Calcutta/Kolkata

Job Charnock's Calcutta
Post- imperial Kolkata
Three villages merge joyously
Gobindopur, Sutanuti, Kalikata
In an inseparable embrace of creation

Calcutta/Kolkata
My cosmopolitan city
Rooted in the soil of rural Bengal
Fusion and effusion
Local and global cultures
In incessant dialogue
Cathedrals, synagogues
Temples and mosques
In peaceful co-existence.

Kolkata you inspire me
Kolkata you shock me
Kolkata you heal me
Kolkata you kill me
Kolkata you love me
Your love makes me persist
Your love makes me insist
That Kolkata is MY city
Though I am a citizen of the world.

Two in One: Calcutta

Three villages conjoined
And a city was born
A river, a busy port, a strand
An Esplanade, a New Market
Everyone's dream mall
A green carpet in the middle of the city
Stretched towards the Race course
The green park, the maidan
Revived the tired minds and limbs
Football, cricket, mounted policemen
Handsome on their black and brown steeds
So alien and so enchanting!

A few kilometres away
Away from Calcutta was its twin
Kolkata, not identical twins
But twins with distinct identities.
Kolkata In the North
Narrow roads, alleys, colonial theatre halls
The mansion of the megastar at Jorasanko
The mellifluous melody of Tagore songs
The waft of misthi from countless sweet shops
Two in one, Calcutta and Kolkata
Two tempting flavours in one cone
Irresistible togetherness
Inseparably entwined.

Cows Blazing

Cows, cows
Blazing bright
In my country day and night
What immortal hand or eye
Could frame thy bovine symmetry?

William Blake's imaginary tiger
TS Eliot's Christ the tiger
Appear in the juvenescence of the year
These thankfully dwell in the mind
They are not seen so nothing to neutralize

The maternal vegetarian cow
Which will never ever know
How glorious it is to be a cow
Just munches and masticates on and on
Wondering why these strange humans are always wrong

For some the masticating, meditative cow
Is a juicy beef steak cooked just not anyhow
For some the same masticating, meditative cow
Is a lactating mother who deserves a wow

No animal has played such a stellar dual role
As the edible FMCG dizzily roll
Beef and milk are in the same food stalls
No one finds this odd in the grocery malls

Smiling in wonder
How cowed we are by cows
Our very own, often emaciated
But sometimes roly-poly holy cow
Whispered with glee
"Wow, its such fun to be an Indian cow"

Balloon

At the start
No one noticed
That the talented star
Brilliance blazing
Like a hundred tropical suns
Or was it like a thousand blast-furnaces
Was slowly but steadily changing
Changing and changing and changing
Till the star became a bombastic gas balloon
The star's orations and odes to himself
Deafened the ears, split the eardrums
Of all those around as well as his own!

The gas balloon floated around
Belted out an earful of "I am supreme" lyrics
In passionate thundering surround sound
Everyone fled as they spotted
The floating , bloated, bombastic balloon

"I can sympathize. I am too brilliant for them"
Smugly smiled the cheeky gas balloon
Outstanding, outlandish orangutan

A superstar's metamorphosis into
A mean megalomaniac bubble
A pompous porpoise poised
On the top rung
Of a descending inexorable escalator!

The Dumb Cow

If only holy cows
Our Moms in distress
Could speak
Instead of carrying on
With their determined silence
For so many centuries
They may have said...
"After being nourished and nurtured
In the wholesome nourishing
Nutritional flowing pure white
Frothy   protein
How can you be so cruel
Brutal and ruthless
Towards others
For some political gain!

No wonder often
Our white streaming milk is curdled
As from cradle to the last journey
Our milk so user-friendly
Is so ill-used and abused
Our oozing milk of human kindness

Our maternal role
Mocked and manipulated
For more barbaric violence
In the name of the Mother Cow!"
Then the cows chanted in a chorus:
"O tempora O mores!
If only we could commit mass suicide
And leave this earth free of cows
We just can't stand our split identity-
Yummy for some
Mummy for others!"

The Hunted
(After watching the web series Delhi Crime in March 2019)

It was just a bus-ride home, Mama
Just a bus ride home at ten that evening
But it was a bus full of hyenas
Six of them, or sixteen or were they sixty
Even my friend pawed me like a hyena
While the others watched, licking their lips
Saliva dripping from their wet, sloppy, lolling tongues

They pounced on me, they stripped me stark
They manhandled my helpless body parts
They bit me, slapped me, twisted my protesting arms
They raped me again and again and again
Into the recess from which one day my baby
Could have slid out into this beautiful world
The iron rod tore through
The terrified tunnel of my trembling body

The rest is history, the police, the hospital
My recorded statements, the protests
I died far away from home

I died far away from my homeland
What a first trip abroad it was for me!

But no, I haven't left
Each winter night in December
You may find me
Standing next to that ditch at midnight
Standing on the lonely bus route
My blood-dripping intestines spilling out!

Tell me what was my mistake
Friends, teachers, parents, politicians and priests?

(These lines refer to the Delhi bus rape case of Nirbhaya (Jyoti Singh) in 2012. The accused are in death row, except the minor)

The four convicts, Akshay, Pawan, Vinay and Mukesh were convicted for raping and brutally torturing 23-year-old paramedic Jyoti Singh on the night of December 16, 2012. A total of six people were convicted, out of which one juvenile was released after a three-year reform facility. The sixth convict, Ram Singh died during the trial.

https://www.indiatoday.in/fyi/story/nirbhaya-gangrape-case-jyoti-singh-convicts-rapists-975462-2017-05-05

Why I am Not a Humanist

That's all crap
This chatter about inclusive human rights
Human rights are exclusive
Human rights are male rights
Women have no human rights!

Why else are innocent women
Eyed as luscious ripe fruits
Munched and squeezed
Till their last breath is wrung out

"Look, look there's that dainty Mina off to high school"
The caterwauling of roadside loafers and drop-outs
Made her blood go cold, anger was the wrong emotion
She learnt, as soon as she had stepped into teenage.
"she has passed out from school. she goes to college now"
An informed smart aleck remarked.

It had been drizzling since morning
Puddles of water made walking very slow.
Two of the guys brushed against her
She lost her balance, as she was falling two others
Lifted her frail body, clamped a hand over her mouth

They carried her into the dark ruined abandoned house
The barbaric torture went on and on
She knew she couldn't fight them off
She cried and screamed
"I'll report you to the police, you will rot in jail
For the rest of your evil lives"

They slapped her hard on the mouth
Blood spurted from her lips
They hit her head with a rock
Was she dead? Was she unconscious?
They tore her limbs apart
They broke her legs
Their knives plunged in and out
Of her quiet body in repose
Her body parts were a jig-saw puzzle
They tossed off the parts over the mossed
Boundary wall into a pond on the other side

The victim of the Kamduni rape case
Haunts my sleep every night
She stalks my every step
'Why, why, why', she asks incessantly

The humanists who were feminists
Raised their clenched fists
"Enough", they thundered
"Our Kamduni sister must be avenged
The humanists must unite with the feminists
 Not fanatic fundamentalists
The world needs empathetic inclusivists!"

Who Killed the Little Tribal Girl?

It was evening in the cold Himalayan hills
"Where are you, come back right now"
Her mother called out
Like she did every evening
"where are you naughty girl
I told you strange animals
Pounce on little kids at this time
Can be a hyena, wild dogs or worse"

But the eight year old girl
 Did not come back home that night
Her brothers and father came back from work
All the villagers of that tiny tribal village
Were back in their huts
But the little girl did not come back home that night

The men older than her father
Had asked her to mop the temple rooms
She entered the abandoned temple
The men older than her father
Pinned her to the floor
Tied her hands and feet

To four posts and began a game
Of hurting and invading every part
Of her spring-chicken like body
Her clothes were torn off and each time she screamed
The men who were older than her father
Grunted and slapped her face
She groaned and moaned
She bled, screamed and cried
The eight year old girl
Just couldn't understand
What adult sport this was
That was pinning, ripping and killing her

Then one of the men older than her father
Did something to her neck
And the terrified tribal girl
Couldn't feel anything anymore

They said, "these unruly tribal kids
She must have been killed by a pack of wild dogs
These filthy low-caste pests are such scums
They claim our land and blame us when they die!"

One Hundred and Fifty Years Young

Ahimsa, ahimsa, ahimsa
Sahansilata, sahridayata
Non-violence, tolerance, empathy
Are these now frozen fossils or dwarfed bonsais
Obsolete words in a forgotten
Dictionary of human values?

He chanted the enchanting song of tolerance
He chanted the alluring anthem for an inclusive world
He sang the song of non-violence
He sang the song of empathy and love
As he chanted the mesmeric anthem
 Raghupati Raghav Raja Ram

'Ishwar-Allah tero naam' was not an oxymoron
It was a joyous juxtaposition
A conscious conjunction
Of hearts and minds and human beings

ईश्वर अल्लाह तेरे नाम
सबको सन्मति दे भगवान...

And then came the darkest morning
In our nation's history
The messiah of non-violence
Died as a victim of violence
He was murdered on a cold January morning
In independent India by an Indian

Many, many, too many
Die even now as victims of violence
Jesus Christ, Joan of Arc
Abraham Lincoln, Martin Luther King,
Indira Gandhi, Rajiv Gandhi, Benazir Bhutto
Murdered by the forces of intolerance
Forces of greed, envy and unbridled lust for power.

But the resonance of the timeless bhajan that he loved so well
Has permeated every pore of our nation's soul
We shall overcome and stand united for we know–

ईश्वर अल्लाह तेरे नाम
सबको सन्मति दे भगवान...

Note: Divinity can be addressed by any name-Ishwar or Allah. The need of the hour is benediction for all.

This perhaps is what the popular song means. It was routinely sung at the prayer meetings organized by Gandhi. It is a song of empathy, tolerance and non-violence.

Protest

There is pin-drop silence all around
But no pin drops
Only bombs with silencers
Drop and implode
Houses and bodies explode
Flesh, bricks and mortar
Lie in tangled blood-drenched heaps
The packed impact
Of brutal carnage and mass murder
Bubble in gleeful celebration of gore

Voices can't be raised
Strangled and gagged
Voices just whimper
Voices parrot the words
That the commander voices

In a strange automated land
Of robots and puppets
Intelligence is chained
By murderous power-brokers
The manipulative mafia snigger and grin

Glued by fear and self-love
Not a single voice rises in protest!

Dress and Address

That was once upon a time
When address and dress
Were always together
The sari, dhoti, lungi and salwar
Signalled like passports
As did the shirts, suits, gowns and frocks
Now passports, address, dress
Are like a Rubik's cube
You can seek but none know if
What you get is what you want!

The global village is about spillage
It is about ruptures and fracture
Mobility of tops and blue jeans
Masquerading in cafes and malls
Despite desperate means
The ravenous vultures of globalization
Have plunged their beaks and claws
Into the carcass of culture,
Footprints have become predatory paws
Myriads of cloned blue jeans swarm and chant
"Identical is a step towards the global
Identity is a step towards the local
Global, local, glocal
Can we have equality
Not just equity in a 50-50 world?"

Dhoti Dance

Those were the days
When it was not about twirling the moustache
It was not about dancing in nightclubs
It was not about challenging the choreographer
It was not about grabbing the chance chance chance
To dance dance dance the lungi dance.

There were no music and drums
As the dhotis and saris
Danced down the streets
To face the imperial rod of power
Soldiers striped their backs
Soldiers handcuffed them
But they sat like boulders

It was the dance of satyagraha
It was a dance of non-violent non-co-operation
That shook the foundations of the British raj

The frail old man in a dhoti led the British such a dance
That their pantaloons and pajamas
Slipped off as they pranced and danced
It was not chance pey dance, it was the determined dhoti dance

The youthful old man had choreographed
 The freedom dance
A nation danced to his tune
A nation danced towards freedom
As Mohandas Karamchand Gandhi
The frail brown man in a capri-dhoti,
Led the dhoti dance.

Note: Poem inspired by the gyrations of the hero in "Lungi dance" a song - dance sequence in the block-buster film Chennai Express (2013)

SANJUKTA DASGUPTA

Dr. Sanjukta Dasgupta, Former Professor and Former Head, Dept of English and Former Dean, Faculty of Arts, Calcutta University is a poet, critic and translator. She is the recipient of numerous national and international grants and fellowships and has lectured, taught and read her poems in India, Europe, USA and Australia. Dasgupta is a member of the General Council of Sahitya Akademi New Delhi, and Convenor of the English Advisory Board, Sahitya Akademi. Her published books include *Snapshots* (poetry), *Dilemma* (poetry), *First Language* (poetry), *More Light* (poetry), *Her Stories* (translations), *Manimahesh* (translation), *Media, Gender and Popular Culture in India: Tracking Change and Continuity*, *SWADES—Tagore's Patriotic Songs* (translation), *Abuse and Other Short Stories, Lakshmi Unbound* (poetry) 2017.